MW01556977

# The Joy of Green Cleaning



## Leslie Reichert

**Certified Green Cleaner**

# The Joy of Cleaning

# A cook book for green cleaning.

My mission is to teach and encourage others in the art of homekeeping and green cleaning, so they can enjoy a good life!

By Leslie Reichert

Cover Design by Carole Donovan
Image Boosters Imageboosters.com

Editing by Jodi Peterson

Photographs used with permission

Illustrations by Lindsey Reichert

Photo enhancements by Richard Ervin Photography   Harwich MA

Cl Publishing

Uxbridge, MA

# ACKNOWLEDGMENTS

For my family, who are my raving fans!

Especially my husband, Austin, who inspired me to "get back in there and make something happen!" Thank you for your love and support.

And to the women in my life that have encouraged me along the way -Mom, Trudy-mom, Jen, Lindsey and all my friends that have worked by me and with me.

A special thank-you to Ann: I still feel your two hands pushing me to do it! Thank-you.

**Leslie, the cleaning coach**

...encourage the young women to love their husbands, to love their children, to be sensible, pure, keepers of the home... so that the word of God will not be dishonored

Titus 3-5

# BACK DOOR

## The Back Door

432 North Main St.

Uxbridge, MA  01569

1-866-50clean

508-234-4626

cleaningcoach.us                    vacuumlady.com

Part of the proceeds of this book will be donated to Peace
of Bread Community Kitchen in Whitinsville, MA



## Do you have a great green recipe…

tip, idea or just a memory you would like to see featured in our next book?
Visit our web site at thecleaningcoach.us and email us to submit your
favorite green cleaning recipe or tip.  Or you can mail them to us at:

The Back Door

Attn: Book Department

432 N. Main St.

Uxbridge, MA  01569

Don't forget to include your name, street address, phone number and e-
mail address. If we select your entry, your name will appear with your
submission… and you will receive a FREE copy of the book!

# Contents

# What is the big deal about greening your cleaning?

Did you know that my great-grandmother cleaned her home with five simple things: white vinegar, lemon juice, salt, baking soda and Borax. In the late 1800's, women spent their entire day trying to get dirt out of their house. My grandmother lived to be very old and she cleaned her whole life without using antibacterial spray, bleach, or all the other things we are told we need to use to keep our homes truly clean.

The truth is that most regular cleaning can be done without any toxic chemicals. Simple things in your panty can do a great job cleaning your home. Baking soda, vinegar, sea salt, lemon juice, and hydrogen peroxide can be used in place of most grocery store cleaners. Or, if you don't want to mix up your own, green companies are creating cleaning products that are made with simple ingredients- and they really work.

One of the questions I receive every day is "How do I disinfect my home?" Honestly, I doubt that we need to do this at all. What we have done recently is try to kill all the bacteria in our homes. Some people don't realize that there are good bacteria and bad bacteria, and the only thing that lives through a cleaning with antibacterial products are the bad bacteria. These bacteria survive and create an even stronger form that is resistant to the antibacterial agents you use to kill them.  So if you think about it, you may be doing more damage to your body by using chemicals than the "bad" bacteria can possibly do to you.

This book contains recipes for cleaners you can use every day in your kitchen, your bathroom, on your floors, in your laundry, and with your furniture using simple products you keep in your pantry. Some of the ingredients, like soap flakes, are rarely produced but we have found suppliers for all of them and have them listed in the back of the book.  (We also have references to products that you can try if you don't want to make your own.)

So go ahead and give it a try! I always love to see the faces of people when I show them what a cut lemon and some salt can really do. You'll be surprised too!

Happy Cleaning!


Leslie Reichert

The Cleaning Coach

cleaningcoach@yahoo.com

# Daily Kitchen Cleaners

# Multi-purpose Cleaner

1 teaspoon borax

½ teaspoon washing soda

2 tablespoon vinegar

½ teaspoon liquid castile soap*

2 cups very hot water

Warm up the water in the microwave for 45 seconds. Add each of the ingredients in small amounts into the hot water. Mix while adding these ingredients. Add the soap last and don't mix it a lot (you don't want a lot of foam.) Rinse thoroughly.

Tools to use: Microfiber cloths, microfiber mop or sparkle sponges*

Non-toxic alternatives: Mrs. Meyers* all-purpose cleaner in different scents, Caldrea* all-purpose cleaner or Bi-o-Kleen* all-purpose cleaner.

**Mrs. Meyer's All Purpose Cleaner**

# All-Purpose Liquid Cleaner

16 ounces of club soda

1 tablespoon baking soda

4 drops dish soap

6 drops any essential oil for fragrance

Mix the dish soap and baking soda together, and then add to the club soda. Add your choice of essential oil. Place into a spray bottle.

This mixture can be used on countertops and floors. It is good for all around cleaning.

To make a heavy duty cleaner, add 3 tablespoons of borax.

**Imus All Purpose Cleaner**

# Daily Counter Cleanser

1 cup white vinegar

1 cup water

8 drops essential oil in lemon scent


Mix the vinegar and water together. Add the oil for a fresh scent. To make the mixture stronger, heat it in the microwave. Use the mixture in a spray bottle.

Tools: Microfiber cloths

**Heinz Distilled
White Vinegar**

# Daily Dish Soap

3 cups castile soap*

16 drops essential oil


Mix the soap with the oil of your choice for a fragrance to fill the kitchen every time you wash a dish. If you have a dispenser that will turn the soap to foam, add 3 cups of water. This can be used for dishes or for hand soap.

# Baking Soda Scrubbing Paste

2 tablespoons baking soda

6 drops dish soap

Water to make paste


Mix the baking soda with the dish soap in small amounts. Add the water to make a thin paste.

Use this paste for difficult areas during cleaning. You can use this to scrub out stainless steel sinks as well as counters and other difficult areas.

Tools: Scrubby sponges, sparkle sponges*, skoy clothes.

Mrs. Meyer's Surface Scrub

# Green Gentle Scrub

This mixture is a great alternative to a commercial "scrub". (Try to avoid using chlorine bleach for cleaning.)

1 cup borax

½ cup salt

Olive oil or dish soap to create paste

6 drops essential oils for fragrance

Create a paste that will act like a liquid scrub for cleaning stains from countertops and in your sink. Rinse thoroughly.

Tools: scrubby sponges, sparkle sponges* fine grade steel wool.

**Casabella Sparkle Sponges**

# Green Powder Scrub

This mixture can be kept in a shaker container by the sink and will act just like any "over the counter" powder cleanser.

1 cup borax

2 cups salt (sea salt for more aggressive cleanser)

2 cups baking soda

8 drops essential oils for fragrance

Mix borax, salt and baking soda thoroughly. After they are completely mixed together, add the essential oils for fragrance.

Keep this mixture in a shaker container with a lid. Use it for cleaning stains on counters and sinks. Rinse thoroughly.

Tools: Skoy cloths* and sponges

# Foaming Sink Cleanser

½ cup baking soda

1 tablespoon cream of tartar

¼ cup vinegar

Mix baking soda and cream of tartar together. Sprinkle them into the sink, lightly covering the bottom. Put vinegar in a spray bottle and spray the entire sink. The mixture will start to foam. Scrub the foam with a scrubby sponge. Rinse completely to remove any leftover film from the baking soda.

Illustration by Lindsey Reichert

# Oven Cleaner

1 cup baking soda

2 cups white vinegar in a spray bottle

Sprinkle the base of the oven with the baking soda. Spray the vinegar over the baking soda to make a light foam. Let the foam sit as long as you can. Keep spraying the baking soda to keep it moist.  For the side of the oven, mix some baking soda with water to make a thick paste and spread on the sides of the oven. Spray the paste with vinegar and leave it sit as long as you can. Wipe off the excess paste and then rinse with hot water.

**Note: If you have a self-cleaning stove you need to check with the manufacturer to make sure you can use this recipe. Self-cleaning ovens have a special coating on the inside and certain elements can damage the coating and ruin the self-cleaning feature. We don't want that!

# Coffeemaker Cleaner

2 cups white vinegar

Run completely through the coffee pot maker. Rinse by running an entire pot of water through the machine.

## Paste for cleaning the coffee pot

¼ cup baking soda

3 tablespoons sea salt

1 teaspoon lemon juice

Mix ingredients to make paste. Rub the inside of the pot with the paste and a skoy cloth*. Rinse thoroughly.


Tip: To clean the inside of a coffee thermos place 3-5 ice cubes inside and sprinkle with salt. Swish and rinse.

# Cutting Board Sanitizer

## Wood Boards

1 lemon/ lime / grapefruit

Small dish of salt

Cut the fruit in half and dip it into salt. Using the salt as a scrub, lightly rub the fruit over the cutting board. Squeeze the fruit as you are rubbing to get the juice to flow. Rinse completely when done.

## Plastic or Glass Boards

¼ cup lemon juice

2 cups water

Let soak for 15 minutes and rinse completely.

# Dishwasher Powder

¼ cup citric acid (Tang drink mix)

1½ cup borax

5 drops castile soap

15 drops essential oil for fragrance


Mix the powders, soap and oil and stir. Keep in an airtight container. Use up to ¼ cup per load of dishes depending on how dirty they are. Always make sure to rinse the dishes if you don't intent to run the washer right away. This keeps the dishwasher smelling fresh and you won't need a lot of dishwashing powder.

# Dishwasher Rinse Aid

½ cup lemon juice

½ cup club soda

2 tablespoons borax

Warm the club soda in the microwave for 30 seconds. Dissolve borax in the club soda, and then add lemon juice. Put into a container with a tapered spout and pour it into the rinse aid dispenser of your dishwasher.

Illustration by Lindsey Reichert

# Stainless Steel – Chrome Polish

1 cup baking soda

¼ cup lemon juice

3 tablespoons borax

Club soda to make paste

Mix baking soda, borax and lemon juice together. Add enough club soda to make paste. Apply the paste to the metal you are cleaning with a soft cloth or skoy cloth*. Rinse with plain club soda. Finish by polishing with a clean cloth.

Tools: Skoy cloth or paper towel to apply paste. Wipe with cotton rags or microfiber cloth.

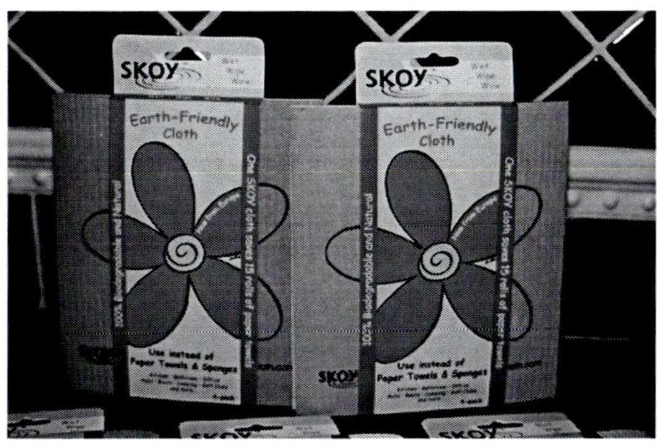


Skoy Cloths

# Metal Cleaners

# Copper Cleaner

¼ cup concentrated lemon juice

¼ cup sea salt

Warm the lemon juice in the microwave for 30 seconds. Then add the sea salt to make a thick paste. Apply to the copper with a microfiber cloth or sponge. Wash with warm water and gentle dish soap. Dry thoroughly with a soft cloth.

## An alternative

¼ cup ketchup

3 tablespoons cream of tartar

Mix ingredients together and rub onto copper. Let sit for 3 to 5 minutes and rinse with warm water. Wash the copper with gentle dish soap and dry with a soft cloth.

# Silver Tarnish Remover

Soak the silver to be cleaned in warm water and 2 cups of salt. Then, using a soft cloth, rub the silver with toothpaste. Use a toothbrush to get into tight areas that need cleaning. Rinse in the sink filled with warm water and 3 teaspoons of baking soda. Use a clean soft cloth to dry.

Cape Cod Silver Polish

# Stainless Steel – Chrome

¼ cup baking soda

¼ cup borax

Lemon juice to make paste

Mix the dry ingredients together. Add enough lemon juice to make a thin paste. Apply to the metal with a sponge or skoy* cloth in a circular motion. Rinse with warm water and a gentle dish soap.

**Seige Stain Steel Cleaner**

# Rust Remover

1 full can of original Coke

This is an amazing solution to removing rust from everything from kitchen utensils to gardening tools. Let the item soak in the can of Coke overnight and it will come out shiny and new.

This will also work for removing rust stains from fixtures in your bathroom. Let it sit overnight in the toilet and you will be rust free!

# Chrome – Copper – Brass

1 whole lemon

1 small dish of sea or regular salt


Cut the lemon in half and dip in the salt. Rub the salt onto the tarnished metal. Squeeze the juice of the lemon out slowly to cover the metal. Once clean, wash in warm water and a gentle dish soap.

# Bathroom Cleaners

# Daily Anti-bacterial Spray

1 cup white vinegar

1 cup club soda

8 drops Tea Tree oil for disinfectant


Mix liquid and put into spray bottle. Add oil for disinfecting properties.


Tools: Use microfiber cloths to pick up bacteria. Wash them in hot water after cleaning to remove bacteria and dirt.

# Anti-bacterial Cleaner

¼ cup soap flakes*

¾ cup hot water

¼ teaspoon baking soda or soda crystals*

¼ teaspoon Tee Tree oil

2 tablespoons isopropyl alcohol (rubbing)


Dissolve the soap flakes in the hot water heated in the microwave for one minute. Slowly add all the other ingredients to the liquid mixture. Place the cleaner in a spray bottle.


Use this mixture to disinfect areas around the toilet and the toilet itself. Use a microfiber cloth to clean the area completely.

**Soap Flakes**

# Bathroom Powder Scrub

1 cup borax

1 cup baking soda

½ cup sea salt

6 drops essential oils for fragrance


Mix all the dry ingredients. Add the essential oils for fragrance. Keep in a shaker container for cleaning the bathroom sink and tub.


Tools: Scrubby sponge, skoy* cloths, sparkle sponge* or sponge.


Tips: Make sure to disinfect your skoy cloths* and sponges in the microwave for 2 minutes (wet) after using on bathroom fixtures.

# Gentle Scrub

¾ cup baking soda or soda crystals*

¼ cup powdered milk

1/8 cup liquid castile soap*

6 drops essential oil for scent

Enough water to make paste

This mixture is great for gently scrubbing extremely sensitive fixtures in your bathroom. Just use the paste with a soft cotton or microfiber cloth.

Soda Crystals

# Tub and Tile Scrub

1 cup borax

½ cup sea salt

½ cup baking soda or soda crystals*

¼ cup olive oil

5 drops dish soap

Club soda


Mix borax, salt and baking soda completely. Add olive oil and dish soap to make a paste. Add club soda until you have a creamy paste. Keep in a container with a screw top lid.


Tools: Scrubby sponge, sparkle sponge*.


Tips: Apply the paste in circular motion and if the tile is stained, leave the paste on for two hours. Then spray the paste with white vinegar to form a foamy rinse. Wipe away the foam with warm water and rinse thoroughly.

# Tile Cleaner

1 cup vinegar

¼ cup borax

1 gallon hot water


Heat the vinegar in the microwave until boiling. Dissolve the borax into the vinegar. Mix the entire solution into a gallon bucket of hot water. Use a stiff brush to wash wall and floor tiles.

Illustration by Lindsey Reichert

# Citrus Tub Scrubber

Great for porcelain tubs

¼ cup baking soda

¼ cup castile soap*

2 vitamin C tablets

Crush the vitamin C tablets until a smooth powder. Add the powder to the castile soap. Then add enough baking soda until you get a smooth paste. Use on a scrubby sponge or skoy* cloth to apply directly to the tub. Apply in a circular motion and leave for a few minutes. Rinse with warm water

# Whitening – Scouring Powder

1 cup baking soda

2 tablespoons cream of tarter

1/8 cup of borax

6 drops of lemon juice or lemon essential oil

Mix all the dry ingredients. Add the oil or juice and place in a shaker container. Use with an abrasive scrubbing sponge or very fine steel wool.

Tips: Mix with a small amount of water to make a paste and let it sit for up to an hour. Scrub in a circular motion and wipe clean.

# Toilet Bowl Powder

1 cup borax

1 cup baking soda or soda crystals*

1 cup salt

6 drops Tea Tree oil for disinfecting

Mix all the dry ingredients. Add the tea tree oil to make powder a disinfecting powder. Use in the toilet with a clean toilet brush. For added cleansing add a cup of white vinegar to the toilet after scrubbing with the powder. Flush.

Tip: Turn off the water to the toilet and flush so all the water empties out of the base. Sprinkle the cleansing powder directly to the porcelain and scrub directly with a scrubby sponge. Add the vinegar and let sit for 1-2 hours then turn on the water and flush. Now you have one clean toilet!

# Toilet / Porcelain Cleaner

2 cups water

¼ cup castile soap* or dish soap

1 teaspoon Tea Tree oil

Mix together and use sparingly in the toilet. To scrub off stains and rings from hard water, use a handled pumice stone*.  Also drain the toilet of the water by turning off the supply line and flushing. This will not dilute the cleaner.

Illustration by Lindsey Reichert

# Mold Scrub

¼ cup vinegar

½ cup borax

3 tablespoons lemon juice

Heat the vinegar and lemon juice in the microwave for 30 seconds. Mix in the borax until it turns into a paste. Use a stiff brush to apply directly to the mold. Let the mixture set to let the acid in the vinegar and lemon juice kill the mold. Then finish scrubbing the area and rinse with warm water.

# Mold Spray

1 teaspoon borax

3 tablespoons vinegar

½ cup hot water

Heat the water in the microwave for 30 seconds. Dissolve the borax in the water, and then add the vinegar. Reheat the entire mixture and put in a spray bottle. Spray directly on the mold and let sit. Wipe the area with a scrubby sponge and then rinse with water and a microfiber cloth.

**Microfiber Cleaning Cloth**

# Foamy Drain Cleaner

1 cup white vinegar

3 tablespoons baking soda


Heat the vinegar in microwave for 1 minute. Pour the baking soda down the drain, followed by the hot vinegar. Let it sit for 10 to 15 minutes. While waiting, heat a pot of hot water and pour down the drain to remove buildup in pipes. Repeat as needed.


Tips: Find a small bottle brush and go down the drain with the brush. You can also try a plunger to remove more of the buildup.

# Grout Cleaner

1 cup Oxygen Bleach*

Hot water to make paste


Mix the oxygen bleach powder with hot water to create thick paste. Using a toothbrush or stiff grout brush, apply the paste to the grout. Let it sit for 1-2 hours. Rinse and repeat if necessary.


Tools: Use a stiff toothbrush, grout brush or wire brush to apply paste. Wash off with a cotton rag or microfiber cloth.

---

1 cup Oxygen Bleach*

# Hair Spray Remover

½ cup fabric softener

½ cup hot water

Mix the two ingredients and put into a spray bottle. Spray directly on hairspray build-up. Let the mixture sit for a few minutes. Wipe with a scrubby sponge.

Tools: Scrubby sponge, sparkle sponge or skoy cloth*.

**Sparkle sponges are safe for fiberglass**

# Glass and Mirror Cleaners

2 tablespoons white vinegar

½ cup cornstarch

2 liter bottle club soda


Mix club soda with cornstarch until dissolved. Add the white vinegar and put into spray bottle. Spray directly to mirrors and inside of windows.

*******************************************

1 cup alcohol in spray bottle

Spray directly to mirrors

*******************************************

1 teaspoon dish soap

½ cup white vinegar

3 cups distilled water

Place all ingredients in spray bottle. Spray directly onto windows and mirrors.

*******************************************

For streak free glass, use a high grade microfiber cloth* with very hot water. It will leave your glass streak free, lint free and will repel dust for days!

# Window Cleaner

To remove Acid Rain Spots:

½ cup vinegar

½ cup lemon juice

Mix together and apply to window with a scrubby sponge or sparkle sponge.

**Microfiber Blue Cloth**

# Bathroom Tile Floor Cleaner

1 cup white vinegar

¼ cup borax

Bucket of hot water


Pour vinegar into bucket of hot water then add borax. Use microfiber cloth or mop to clean tile floor.


Tips: Mix ¼ cup vinegar, 3 tablespoons borax and 16 ounces hot water then place in a spray bottle. Spray directly to floor and wipe with microfiber cloth or mop.

# Bathroom Floor Cleaner

¼ cup lemon juice

8 drops dish soap

3 tablespoons skim milk or dry powdered milk


Mix the ingredients with 16 ounces of warm water and put into a spray bottle. Spray directly onto floor and use a wet cloth or wet microfiber cloth to clean the floor. Rinse if needed.

# Floor Cleaners

# No Wax Floor Cleaner

¼ cup lemon juice

8 drops dish soap

3 tablespoons skim milk or dry powdered milk


Mix the ingredients with 16 ounces of warm water and put into a spray bottle. Spray directly onto floor using a wet cloth or wet microfiber cloth to clean the floor. Rinse if needed. This method does not need a bucket. You will use less cleaner and less water.

# Grout Cleaner

1 cup Oxygen Bleach*

Hot water to make paste


Mix the oxygen bleach powder with hot water to create thick paste. Using a toothbrush or stiff grout brush, apply the paste to the grout. Let it sit for 1-2 hours. Rinse and repeat if necessary.


Tools: Use a stiff toothbrush, grout brush or wire brush to apply paste. Wash off with a cotton rag or microfiber cloth.

# Hardwood Floor Cleaner

1 teaspoon dish soap

1 cup white vinegar

16 ounces hot water


Mix all ingredients and place in a spray bottle. Use a dry microfiber mop after vacuuming the hardwood floor. Spray the floor with cleaner and wipe with the dry microfiber mop. This mixture will leave the floor, clean without a waxy buildup.

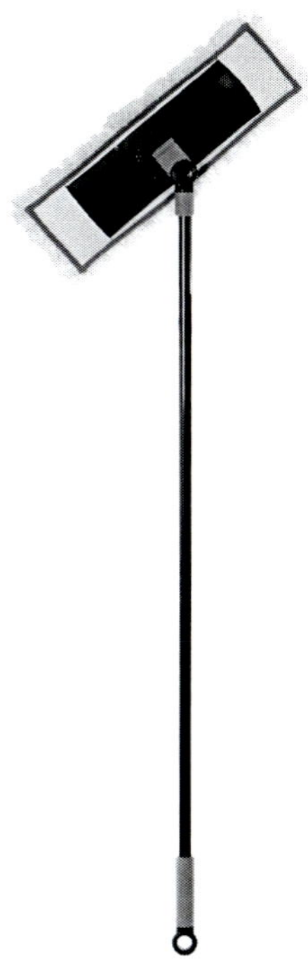

**Microfiber Mop**

# Tile Floor Cleaner

1 cup white vinegar

¼ cup borax

Bucket of hot water


Pour the vinegar into bucket of hot water then add borax. Use microfiber or sponge mop to clean tile floor.


Tip: The best way to clean floors is on your hands and knees. The next best way is with a microfiber mop. It will make it look like you cleaned on your knees.

# Furniture Care

# Lemony Furniture Re-newer

This mixture is great for old or dried wood furniture. It will also bring back a glow to dark woods.

3 tablespoons lemon juice concentrate

3 tablespoons olive oil

Mix together thoroughly and put on a clean cloth. Wipe the piece of furniture with the grain of the wood. Let the mixture sit for 15 minutes, then wipe the excess off with a clean cotton cloth. (cotton baby diapers (unfolded) are perfect for your furniture.)

# Lemon Furniture Polish

¼ cup olive oil

¼ cup white vinegar

¼ c lemon juice concentrate


Mix the lemon juice and vinegar together first, and then add olive oil. Place mixture on clean cloth and rub into the wood, going with the grain. Let it sit for a few minutes. The furniture will look very dull and smeary. Buff with a clean soft cloth and watch your furniture shine. Wipe off excess oil.

# Light Dusting Spray

This mixture can be used to just lightly dust furniture. It is great for removing pollen.

2 regular tea bags

1 tablespoon lemon juice

3 cups water


Place the 3 cups of water in the microwave for 2 minutes or until boiling. Put both tea bags into the hot water for 2 minutes. While leaving the tea bags in the water, pour yourself one cup of tea, and go relax for a while. Leave the tea bags in the water until the entire mixture has cooled completely. Squeeze out tea bags and place cooled tea in spray bottle. Using a soft cloth, spray the mixture onto the cloth and dust.

# Awesome Furniture Restorer

This recipe is great for dried wood on furniture or just to give it a new luster. It will clean the wood as well as polish. You need to leave some time to do this procedure, as it is a polish and not just for dusting. I would recommend doing this every six months to keep your furniture in its best condition.

¼ cup mayonnaise (regular, not fat free)

¼ cup olive oil

3 tablespoons lemon juice

Mix the mayonnaise and olive oil in a small bowl. Add the lemon juice. Apply the mixture with a small sponge or skoy* cloth. Let it sit for a few minutes. Wipe off excess with a clean soft cloth.

Illustration by Lindsey Reichert

# Laundry Care

# Great-grandma's Laundry Soap

2 cups soap flakes*

1 cup baking soda or soda crystals*

1 cup borax

1 cup washing soda


Mix all the ingredients thoroughly, and then place in plastic or glass container with a lid. This soap works best with hot water.

For top loading washing machines- use ½ to 1 cup, 2 cups for very heavily soiled clothing.

For front loading and HE machines, use 2 tablespoons.

**Great-Grandma Baker**

# Liquid Laundry Soap

1 cup soap flakes*

¼ cup baking soda or soda crystals*

½ cup borax

2 tablespoons glycerin

2 cups water

Mix all the dry ingredients thoroughly. Heat the water in the microwave until boiling (2 minutes), and then mix in dry ingredients. Store the liquid in a plastic airtight container like a milk carton.

**Original Soap Flakes**

# Fabric Softener

3 cups white vinegar

½ cup water

½ cup baking soda

8 drops of your favorite essential oil


Mix the water and the vinegar, and then heat in the microwave for 60 seconds. Dissolve the baking soda into the mixture. Add your choice of essential oils. Use in your wash, just like any store bought liquid fabric softener.


## Alternatives

Add ½ cup of white vinegar, baking soda or borax to the rinse cycle to soften the water and reduce static cling.


Non-toxic alternative – Mrs. Meyers' dryer sheets and Mrs. Meyers' Fabric Softener.


**Tip**: Test your dryer filter for an invisible build-up by running it under water. If it holds water, place it in the dishwasher to remove the build up and then try to switch to a fabric softener that has less wax and oil. This will protect your dryer from over-heating as well as protect your home from an accidental dryer fire.

# Laundry Bleach

¼ cup borax

¼ cup vinegar

¼ cup hydrogen peroxide

Heat the vinegar in the microwave for 30 seconds. Dissolve the borax into the vinegar, and then add the peroxide right before adding to the wash. The peroxide will not stay **active** for very long so you add it to the mixture right before using it.

**Charlie's Soap All Natural
Laundry Soap**

# Other Green Ideas

# Horizontal Blind Cleaner

1 small bottle of club soda

1 microfiber cloth or glove

Find a spray bottle and place the club soda into the spray bottle. Spray a microfiber cloth with the club soda and wipe gently over the blinds. This mixture is for removing a light film of dust, not a heavy build up.

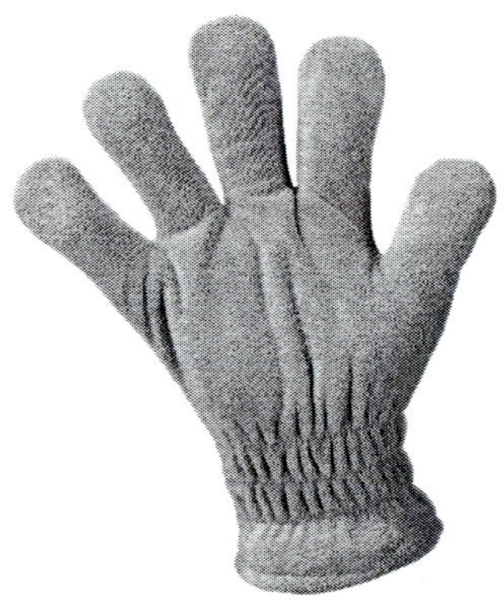

Casabella Microfiber Glove

# Green Shoe Polish

To add a nice shine to shoes use a banana peel and wipe over the shoe. Polish with a thick microfiber cloth.

**Microfiber Cleaning Cloth**

# Leather Conditioner

½ cup olive oil

¼ cup plain brewed tea

¼ cup white vinegar

Combine all three ingredients and place into a spray bottle. Shake well and spray a soft cloth or microfiber cloth with the mixture. Apply lightly to the leather. Let sit for 5 minutes and wipe up any extra.

**Seige Leather Cleaner**

# Green Carpet Freshener

½ cup baking soda

½ cup borax

10 drops essential oil in lemon

Mix the dry ingredients and then add the essential oils. Place in a shaker container and shake onto the carpet whenever it smells stale. Vacuum up carefully as the powder can leak out of the vacuum bag and damage the motor of your vacuum. You may want to use a "shop vac" to vacuum up most of the powder, and then finish with your household vacuum cleaner.

# Carpet Spot Wipes

¼ cup vinegar

¼ cup club soda

8 drops essential oil in lemon


Combine all the ingredients. Soak 20 heavy (microwavable) paper towels in the mixture. Squeeze out the excess and store in a zip lock bag. Use for spots and spills when needed.

# Where to buy it?

One of the problems with "green recipes" is that they list ingredients you may not be able to find. Well we found them for you! Here are the "star*" items in our book.

**Liquid castile soap** - vermontsoap.com, vacuumlady.com or The Back Door – 866-50clean

**Soda Crystals** –soap-flakes.com, vacuumlady.com or The Back Door – 866-50clean

**Soap Flakes** – soap-flakes.com, vacuumlady.com or The Back Door – 866-50clean

**Oxygen Bleach** – bi-o-kleen.com, vacuumlady.com, mrsmeyers.com or The Back Door – 1-866-50clean

**Imus All-Purpose Cleaner**- imusranchfoods.com, vacuumlady.com or The Back Door 1-866-50clean

**Cape Cod Silver Polish** – capecodpolish.ca, vacuumlady.com or The Back Door – 1-866-50clean

**Charlie's Soap** – charliesoap.com, vacuumlady.com or The Back Door 1-866-50clean

**Essential Oils** - the Back Door, vacuumlady.com or Vermontsoap.com

**Freshwave Odor Neutralizer** – fresh-wave.com, vacuumlady.com or The Back Door 1-866-50clean

**Microfiber cloths**- window- all-purpose - dusting - The Back Door 1-866-50clean

**Microfiber mops** – hardwood and tile – casabella.com or The Back Door 1-866-50clean

**Microfiber dusting glove** – casabella.com, vacuumlady.com or The Back Door – 1-866-50clean

**Mrs. Meyer's Products**– mrsmeyers.com, vacuumlady.com, Whole Foods Market or The Back Door 1-866-50clean

**Skoy Cloths** – skoycloth.com, vacuumlady.com or The Back Door 1-866-50clean

**Seige Products** – Seigechemical.com or vacuumlady.com

**Sparkle Sponges** – casabella.com, vacuumlady.com or The Back Door 1-866-50clean

# The Cleaning Coach's Recommended Reading

Yankee Magazine's:  Vinegar, Duct Tape, Milk Jugs & More
By Earl Proulx

Clean Naturally: recipes for body, home and spirit
By Sandy Maine

The Naturally Clean Home
By Karyn Siegel-Maier

How Clean Is Your House: Hundreds of handy tips to make your home sparkle.
By Kim Woodburn and Aggie MacKenzie

The Queen of Clean's Compete Cleaning Guide
By Linda Cobb

Laundry: The Spirit Of Keeping Home
By Monica Nassif

Homekeeping Handbook
By Martha Stewart

Green Guide: The resource for consuming wisely-magazine
thegreenguide.com

---

# Want more?

Call us at our green cleaning hotline at

## 1-866-50clean

We will send you our our latest catalog filled with the best green cleaning products in the world. We carry the very best vacuums, cleaning tools and a full line of green cleaning products.

Phone us: 1-866-50clean

Fax us: 1-508-234-4626

Visit our website: thecleaningcoach.us and our store at vacuumlady.com

# Do you have a favorite great green recipe…

tip, idea or just a memory you would like to see featured in our next book? Visit our web site at thecleaningcoach.us and email us to submit your favorite green cleaning recipe or tip.  Or you can mail them to us at:

The Back Door

Attn: Book Department

432 N. Main St.

Uxbridge, MA  01569

Don't forget to include your name, street address, phone number and e-mail address. If we select your entry, your name will appear with your submission… and you will receive a FREE copy of the book!

# Who is Leslie Reichert, the Cleaning Coach?

Leslie Reichert is a "green" cleaning coach and the owner of the Back Door—a vacuum and homekeeping store now celebrating 18 years in Uxbridge, Massachusetts and nationally online at vacuumlady.com.

For years Leslie supervised a large residential cleaning service in the Blackstone Valley, MA. After cleaning 100-150 homes a week Leslie saw what harsh chemicals could do to your body--and she learned about the green alternatives that do work to clean your home.

Leslie has also seen, firsthand, scores of parents who fight a daily battle with asthma and allergies, which many believe are caused by using harsh chemicals in the home. Three years ago she realized she wanted to share her knowledge and encourage people in the "art" of homekeeping and green cleaning and since then she has become a coach, a presenter, and a speaker for the green cleaning industry. She speaks to groups large and small, does in- home demonstrations on green cleaning, and presents at events such as the Chicago International Home and Housewares Show.

## THREE GOOD REASONS TO GREEN YOUR CLEANING

**For yourself**- To protect your body from chemicals it is simply not designed to process. There may be a correlation to the severe increase in cancers in the waste processing areas of our bodies and the chemicals we use in our homes.

**For your family**- Chemicals used in the home stay in the home--they just don't disappear after you're done cleaning. They can seep into your body through your skin, in fact, veterinarians tell us that chemicals can actually go through the pads of small dogs and cats and can damage their liver and kidneys. Fumes from toxic cleaning products can also linger for months since homes today are energy efficient.

**For the Earth**- By using green cleaning products, you help the waterways and air quality and turn away from Petro-based chemicals made from a non-renewable source.

Want more information? Contact Leslie directly at 1-508-234-4626 or at cleaningcoach@yahoo.com. You can also sign up for free cleaning tips at thecleaningcoach.us.

# Common Hazardous Ingredients in Cleaning Products

## From   http://www.lesstoxicguide.ca

**Acetone-** A neurotoxin, acetone may cause liver and kidney damage, and damage to the developing fetus. It is a skin and eye irritant. Found I spot treatment cleaner, mark and scuff removers and other products.

**Aerosol products-** Aerosol propellants may contain propane, formaldehyde, a carcinogen, neurotoxin and central nervous system depressant, methylene chloride, a carcinogen, neurotoxin and reproductive toxin, and nitrous oxide. Products applied with aerosol sprays are broken in minute particles, which can be more deeply inhaled than larger particles, which may increase their toxic effect.

**Ammonia-** Undiluted, ammonia is a severe eye and respiratory irritant that can cause severe burning pain, and corrosive damage including burns, cataracts and corneal damage. It can cause kidney and liver damage. Repeated or prolonged exposure to vapors can results in bronchitis and pneumonia. Found in a wide range of cleaning products. Ammonia will react with bleach to form poisonous chlorine gas that can cause burning and watering of eyes, as well as burning of the nose and mouth.

**Bleach-** See sodium hypochlorite

**Diethanolamine (DEA)-** Listed as a suspected carcinogen by the state of California, this chemical is a skin and respiratory toxicant and sever eye irritant. Used in a wide range of household cleaning products.

**D-limonene-** This chemical is produced by cold-pressing orange peels, the extracted oil is 90% d-limonene. It is a sensitizer, a neurotoxin, a moderate eye and skin irritant, and can trigger respiratory distress when vapors are inhaled by sensitive individuals. There is some evidence of carcinogencity. D-limonene is the active ingredient in some insectides. It is used as a solvent in many all-purpose cleaning products, especially 'citrus' and 'orange' cleaners. Also listed on labels as citrus and orange oil.

**Ethoxylated nonyl phenol:** Nonyl phenols are hormone disruptors and some contain traces of ethylene oxide, a known human carcinogen. They are eye and skin irritants. Used in laundry detergents and other cleaning products.

**Formaldehyde-** In lab tests, formaldehyde has caused cancer and damaged DNA. Formaldehyde is also a sensitizer, with the potential to cause asthma. Several laboratory studies have shown it to be central nervous system depressant. Exposure to formaldehyde may cause joint pain, depression, headaches, chest pains, ear infections, chronic fatigue, dizziness and loss of sleep. While formaldehyde naturally occurs in the human body in minute amounts, it is estimated that 20% of people exposed to it will experience an allergic reaction. Used in a wide range of products, including some furniture polishes, formaldehyde may be released by other chemicals.

**Fragrance-** Fragrance on a label can indicate the presence of up to 4,000 separate ingredients, most of which are synthetic. Many compounds in fragrance are human toxins and suspected or proven carcinogens. In 1989, the US National Institute of Occupational Safety and Health evaluated 2,983 fragrance chemicals for health effects. They identified 884 of them as toxic substances. Synthetic fragrances are known to trigger asthma attacks. The US Environmental Protection Agency found that 100% of perfumes contain toluene, which can cause liver, kidney and brain damage as well as damage to a developing fetus. Symptoms reported to the FDA from fragrance exposure have included headaches, dizziness, rashes, skin discoloration, violent coughing and vomiting, and allergic skin irritation. Clinical observations by medical doctors have shown that exposure to fragrances can affect the central nervous system, causing depression, hyperactivity, irritability, inability to cope, and other behavior changes. Fragrance is a common skin irritant.

**Methylene chloride-** Methylene chloride is a carcinogen, a neurotoxin and a reproductive toxin. On inhalation, it can cause liver and brain damage, irregular heartbeat and even heart attack. It is a severe skin and moderate eye irritant, it is found primarily in stain removers.

**Monoethanolamine-** This chemical may cause liver, kidney, and reproductive damage, as well as depression of the central nervous system. Inhalation of high concentrations – when cleaning an oven for example – can cause dizziness or even coma. The chemical can also be absorbed through the skin. It is a moderate skin irritant, and a sever eye irritant. Found in many cleaning products, including oven cleaners, tub and tile cleaners, laundry pre-soaks, floor striper and carpet cleaners.

**Morpholine-** This corrosive ingredient can severely irritate and burn skin and eyes, and can even cause blindness if splashed in eyes. It can cause liver and kidney damage, and long-term exposure can result in bronchitis. It reacts with nitrites (added as a preservative in some products, or present as a contaminant) to form carcinogenic nitrosomines. Morphline is moderate to severe eye, skin and mucous membrane irritant. Used as a solvent in a number of cleaning products, including some furniture polishes and abrasive cleansers.

**Naphthalene-** This registered pesticide is listed as a suspected carcinogen in California and is most commonly found in mothballs, and some other pest repellants, as well as in deodorizers. As a reproductive toxin, it is transported across the placenta and can cause blood damage. It can cause liver and kidney damage, and corneal damage and cataracts. Skin exposure is especially dangerous to newborns.

**Parabens-** Parabens are hormone disruptors. Widely used in cleaning products as preservatives, paraben is usually preceded by the prefixes methyl-, ethyl-, butyl-, or propyl. Parabens may cause contact dermatitis in some individuals.

**Paradichlorobenzene** – This highly volatile registered pesticide is in the same chemical class as DDT. It is a suspected carcinogen, and may cause lung, liver and kidney damage. It is used in mothballs and some washroom deodorizers and urinal blocks.

**Phosphoric acid-** Extremely corrosive, it can severely irritate and burn the skin and eyes. Breathing vapors can make the lungs ache, and it may be toxic to the central nervous system.

Fund in some liquid dishwasher detergents, metal polishes, and some disinfectants, and bathroom cleaners, especially those that remove lime and mildew.

**Sodium dichloroisocyanurate dihydrate-** This corrosive chemical is a severe eye, skin and respiratory irritant. It may cause liver and gastrointestinal damage, and may be toxic to the central nervous system It will react with bleach to form poisonous chloride gas that can cause burning and watering of eyes, as well as burning of the nose and mouth. It is found in some toilet bowl cleaners and deodorizers, as well as industrial detergents and some institutional dishwashing detergents.

**Sodium hypochlorite ( bleach) –** A corrosive chemical, sodium hypochlorite is an eye, skin and respiratory irritant, as well as a sensitizer. It is especially hazardous to people with heart conditions or asthma, and can be fatal if swallowed. It may be a neurotoxin and toxic to the liver. Found in a wide range of household cleaners.

**Sodium Lauryl Sulfate-** Sodium lauryl sulfare (SLS) is used as a lathering agent. This chemical is a known skin irritant. It also enhances the allergic response to other toxins and allergens. The U.S government has warned manufacturers of unacceptable levels of dioxin formation in some products containing this ingredient. SLS can react with other ingredients to form cancer-causing nitrosamines.

**Toulene-** Exposure to toluene may cause liver, kidney and brain damage. It is also a reproductive toxin which can damage a developing fetus.

**Turpentine-** This chemical can cause allergic sensitization, kidney, bladder and central nervous damage. Turpentine is an eye irritant, it is found in specialty solvent cleaners, furniture polish and shoe products.

**Xylene-** Xylene has significant neurotoxic effects, including loss of memory. High exposure can lead to loss of consciousness and even death. Xylene has been known to cause damage to the liver, kidney and to the developing fetus. It is a severe eye and moderate skin irritant. Used in some spot removers, floor polishes, ironing aids and other products.

# Great Green Ideas